Robins

Robins

Sharon Sharth

THE CHILD'S WORLD®, INC.

Library of Congress Cataloging-in-Publication Data
Sharth, Sharon.
Robins / by Sharon Sharth.
p.   cm.
Includes index.
Summary: Describes the physical characteristics.
behavior, habitat, and life cycle of robins.
ISBN 1-56766-596-9 (lib. bdg. : alk paper)
1. Robins—Juvenile literature.
[1. Robins.]   I. Title.
QL696.P288S48   1999
598.8'42—dc21   98-31200
CIP
AC

Photo Credits

© A. & S. Carey/VIREO: 19
© Alan & Sandy Carey: cover, 2, 6, 20, 24
© Daniel J. Cox/Natural Exposures, Inc.: 9
© Dwight R. Kuhn: 16
© Gene Boaz: 26
© 1993 Gijsbert van Frankenhuyzen/Dembinsky Photo Assoc. Inc.: 30
© 1994 John Mielcarek/Dembinsky Photo Assoc. Inc.: 10
© Leonard Lee Rue III, The National Audubon Society Collection/Photo Researchers: 23
© Maslowksi, The National Audubon Society Collection/Photo Researchers: 15
© 1998 Rolf Kopfle/Dembinsky Photo Assoc. Inc.: 29
© Steven Holt/Aigrette: 13

On the cover...

Front cover: This *American robin* is looking for food on a lawn in Michigan.
Page 2: This female American robin is sitting on her nest in Montana.

Table of Contents

Early in the morning, a bird sings. It takes three little hops across a lawn. The red feathers on its belly stand out against the green grass. Soon its gray head bobs up and down as it pulls on a fat, slimy worm. What is this busy little bird? It's a robin!

⇐ This American robin has just pulled a worm from the ground.

What Are Robins?

Robins are part of a group of birds called **thrushes.** Thrushes are known for their musical singing. Like some other birds, thrushes move from one place to another in the spring and fall. This movement is called **migration.** Most thrushes fly south during the winter to find warmer weather. They travel north again in the spring to have their babies.

This American robin is sitting in a crab apple tree in Minnesota. ⇒

Most robins have dark gray or black bodies. On their chests and bellies, robins often have red or orange feathers. Adults have a white circle around each eye, too.

Robins have four toes—three in front and one in back. The long back toe helps them hang on tight when they sit, or **perch,** on a branch or wire. But robins spend much of their time on the ground. That's where they search for worms and insects!

⇐ It is easy to see how a robin's toes help it to hold onto things.

Are There Different Kinds of Robins?

There are many different kinds of robins. Each type looks a little different from the others. *European robins* have orange faces and bellies. *Bush robins* have red feathers under their wings. The *clay-colored robin* doesn't have any bright feathers at all. It is a dull yellow. The *blackbush robin* is different, too. Its feathers are black and white.

This *clay-colored robin* is sitting on a branch in Mexico. ⇒

Where Do Robins Live?

Robins can be found almost anywhere. They make their homes in cities or in the mountains. They can be found in forests, meadows, and parks. Robins can even be found in backyards! Robins sleep, or **roost,** with other robins in large groups. These groups are called **flocks.** Flocks of robins often cluster together in the branches of tall trees.

This flock of American robins is feeding in a park in Ohio. ⇒

Robins love to eat. They like to catch worms, beetles, spiders, and caterpillars. Flies, moths, and mosquitoes are favorite foods, too. They also eat berries and other wild fruits that they find. Before they migrate, robins eat a lot. The food gives them energy and keeps them strong and healthy during the long trip.

⇐ This young American robin has just caught a worm to eat.

How Are Baby Robins Born?

In the spring, robins migrate north to have their babies. The male flies north before the female. He picks out a home area, or **territory.** This is where he and his partner will eat, sleep, and raise their young. The male often goes back to the exact same place where he nested the year before. He may even find last year's nest! He sings a warbling song to warn other birds to stay away from his territory. He also calls to attract the female robin.

This male American robin is singing on a post within his territory. ⇒

After the male and female robin mate, the female builds a nest. Most of the time, robins make their nests in trees or bushes. Sometimes, though, they build them in strange places, such as under rocks or in garages. The female robin does most of the work building the nest. The male helps by bringing her twigs and weeds. Clumps of fresh grass make the nest soft for the eggs.

When the nest is ready, the female lays three to five blue eggs. She sits on the eggs to keep them warm and safe. Two weeks later, the eggs hatch.

⇐ These robin eggs are safely hidden in the nest their parents made.

What Are Baby Robins Like?

Baby robins are called **chicks.** When robin chicks hatch, they have no feathers and they can't see. They peep and squawk to let their parents know they're hungry. Both parents collect worms and insects for the babies.

The chicks grow quickly. Soon they have soft, downy feathers. Within two weeks, the baby robins leave the nest. They still aren't ready to be on their own, so the father takes over the care of the chicks. Then the mother lays more eggs!

The parents of these hungry chicks work hard to bring them food. ⇒

Robins have lots of enemies. Crows and hawks swoop down on robins from the sky. Cats sneak up on robins and grab them on the ground. Snakes and jays invade their nests, too. To stay safe, robins have learned lots of tricks.

When an enemy is near, robins make a barking call as loud as they can. They fluff up their chest feathers to look bigger. If everything goes right, the enemy gets scared and leaves the robin alone.

⇐ This robin is puffing up its feathers to look bigger.

When an enemy is close to a robin's chicks, the parent flies up into the air. Then it swoops down on the enemy—WHOOSH! The enemy quickly learns that it should leave the chick alone.

Robins also hide to stay safe. Their dark feathers blend in with the grass and leaves around them. This protective coloring is called **camouflage.** As an enemy comes near, robins often crouch under plants and leaves. Their dark upper feathers make them hard to see, and the enemy passes right by.

⇐ It is hard to see this American robin as it stands in the grass.

How Can You Learn About Robins?

Robins can often be found on grassy areas or lawns. If you see robins in your yard, put out a birdbath. Then watch as the robins splash and play in the water. If you don't have a yard, go to a green park. Sit quietly and watch as robins hunt for their food. Be careful not to scare them, though. The robins might think you are an enemy and fly away.

This American robin has caught a fat caterpillar to eat. ⇒

Robins are common birds that have been around for a long time. There have even been stories and poems written about them! To make sure robins stay safe and healthy, we must keep the environment clean. By taking care of the places where robins eat and sleep, we can make sure that these beautiful birds will be around for many years to come.

Glossary

camouflage (KAM–oo–flazh)
Camouflage is the colorings or markings that help an animal hide. Robins' coloring acts as camouflage.

chicks (CHIKS)
Chicks are baby birds. Robin chicks are born blind and without feathers.

flocks (FLOKS)
Flocks are groups of animals that travel, eat, and sleep together. Robins often sleep in flocks.

migration (my–GRAY–shun)
A migration is a move from one place to another. Robins migrate south to warmer regions during the winter.

perch (PERCH)
When a bird perches, it stops to rest. Robins often perch on branches and wires.

roost (ROOST)
When robins sleep, they roost. Robins usually roost in trees.

territory (TARE–ih–tor–ree)
A territory is an area an animal claims as its own. Robins guard their territories carefully.

thrushes (THRUH–shez)
Thrushes are a family of birds known for their beautiful singing. Robins are thrushes.

Index